# The Hermetic and Alchemical Writings of Paracelsus

*Unlocking the Secrets of Nature and Transformation*

## A Modern Translation

Adapted for the Contemporary Reader

## Paracelsus

# Preface - Message to the Reader

### Rebuilding the Greatest Library in Human History

Thousands of years ago, the Library of Alexandria was the heart of global knowledge — a sanctuary where the wisdom of every known civilization was gathered and shared freely.

And then, it was lost.

Now, we're rebuilding it — and you are invited to join us.

At the Library of Alexandria, we've set out to make every book available to *every person on Earth* — not just in print, but in every language, every format, and for every reader.

Here's how we do it:

- **Deluxe Print Editions at True Printing Cost** - Order any book as a high-quality paperback, elegant hardcover, or stunning boxset — and only pay what it costs to print. No markups. No middlemen.

- **Unlimited Access to the Greatest Works** - Enjoy thousands of timeless classics — from Plato to Shakespeare to Tolstoy — in beautiful, modern eBook and audiobook editions. Read and listen without limits — for every reader, everywhere.

- **Modern Translations for Every Language & Dialect** - We're reimagining the classics in clear, accessible language — and translating them into every dialect imaginable. Everyone deserves to understand humanity's greatest ideas.

When you visit **LibraryofAlexandria.com**, you're not just accessing books — you're joining a global movement to restore, preserve, and share the wisdom of civilization.

**Join us today at LibraryofAlexandria.com**

Together, we'll ensure the light of human wisdom never fades again.

With gratitude,
**The Modern Library of Alexandria Team**

**Visit:**

**www.libraryofalexandria.com**

**Or scan the code below:**

# Table of Contents

# Foreword

This is a collection of five alchemical writings by one of the most renowned alchemists, believed to have discovered the Philosopher's Stone. In these texts, Paracelsus tries to explain the nature of the Philosopher's Stone and the scientific principles that confirm its existence and reveal how it works. Like many alchemical writings, the language used is intentionally cryptic and symbolic, making it difficult for those considered unworthy to understand.

• • •

# About the Author

## Paracelsus (1493 – 1541)

Paracelsus was an alchemist, physician, astrologer, and occultist, born in Einsiedeln, Switzerland. His birth name was Phillip von Hohenheim, but he later adopted the name Philippus Theophrastus Aureolus Bombastus von Hohenheim. Eventually, he began using the title Paracelsus, meaning "equal to or greater than Celsus," a Roman writer from the first century known for his work on medicine.

Paracelsus authored many writings on alchemy, focusing primarily on the nature of the Philosopher's Stone. Unfortunately, he met an early and violent end, killed by those who were envious of his superior knowledge and irritated by his arrogant demeanor.

• • •

# Prologue to The English Translation

You, who are skilled in Alchemy, along with others who hope to gain great wealth or dream of making gold and silver through its promises, take note. Many of you willingly endure hard work and frustrations, refusing to give up until you reach the rewards you believe this art will bring. Yet, experience shows that out of thousands, hardly one person achieves their goal. Is this failure caused by Nature or by Art? I say, no. It is instead due to fate or the lack of skill on the part of the alchemist.

Since those familiar with this art already understand the symbols, star signs, and planetary influences, as well as the ingredients, tools, and instructions, there is no need to repeat them here. These elements still serve a purpose when used at the right time, but this book offers a new way of approaching Alchemy. It will be explained through Seven Canons, following the order of the seven metals. Although this approach avoids unnecessary words, these Canons cover everything that should be separated from Alchemy. They also reveal many hidden secrets and insights into other areas of knowledge. In fact, this method may challenge the ideas of older alchemists and philosophers, but it is backed by careful testing and experimentation.

The most important truth in this art, though little known and rarely trusted, is that failure in Alchemy comes entirely from a lack of skill or using the wrong amounts or types of materials. Many people are driven to poverty, while others waste their efforts simply because of these mistakes. Success comes only when the process is done correctly, and if followed precisely, the substance being transformed steadily moves closer to perfection each day. The right path is simple, but only a few ever find it.

Sometimes, an alchemist may try to invent a new method out of curiosity, whether it works or not. But he need not try to create something out of nothing— or turn something into nothing—just for the sake of it. Even so, there is truth in the saying: "Destruction reveals what is good." This is because the good remains hidden beneath what covers it. Until this covering is removed, the good cannot shine in its full brightness. For example, a metal hidden within a mountain, sand, earth, or stone cannot reveal itself until its covering is removed. In the same way, each visible metal conceals the presence of the other six metals.

Through the element of fire, everything that is flawed or imperfect is destroyed and removed—such as the five metals associated with Mercury, Jupiter, Mars, Venus, and Saturn. However, the perfect metals, Sol (gold) and Luna (silver), do not burn up in this same fire. Instead, they remain in the fire, and from the destruction of the other imperfect metals, these perfect ones take shape and become visible. The way this transformation happens is explained in the Seven Canons. From these Canons, you can learn the nature and properties of each metal, how they interact with one another, and what powers they have when combined.

It's important to understand right from the beginning that these Seven Canons cannot be fully grasped on a quick read or after just one attempt. Complex and hidden ideas are not easy for everyone to comprehend. Each Canon requires thoughtful study and discussion. Many people, filled with pride, assume they can easily understand everything in this book. They dismiss its contents as worthless, believing they have better ideas of their own and so do not value what is written here.

• • •

# Coelum Philosophorum

*The Secrets of Alchemy, Nature, and Spiritual Wisdom*

## A Modern Translation

Adapted for the Contemporary Reader

## Paracelsus

Translated by Tim Zengerink

# Part I

## CONCERNING THE NATURE AND PROPERTIES OF MERCURY

All things are hidden within everything. One thing among them acts as the container for the rest—their physical, visible, and moveable vessel. This vessel reveals all processes of melting or liquefying. It is a living, physical spirit, and when it holds something solid or frozen inside it, those things become restless, wanting to escape. There is no proper name for this process of liquefaction, nor for where it originates. Since no natural heat can match it, it is compared to the fire of Gehenna. This kind of liquefaction is entirely different from those caused by ordinary heat or solidified by cold. Such weak transformations have no effect on Mercury, who rejects them altogether.

From this, we understand that earthly elements, in their destructive processes, cannot add to or take away from celestial powers, which are known as Quintessence or its elements. These higher forces are beyond the influence of earthly elements and cannot be controlled by them. Celestial and infernal forces do not obey the four basic elements—dry, moist, hot, or cold. None of these elements can act against a Quintessence. Each higher power holds its own abilities and operates independently, without needing to rely on the elements.

. . .

# Concerning The Nature and Proper- Ties of Jupiter

Within what is visible—specifically, the body of Jupiter—the other six physical metals are spiritually hidden, though each one is concealed with varying degrees of depth and strength. Jupiter does not contain any Quintessence in its makeup but consists of the four basic elements. Because of this, it melts under moderate heat and solidifies under moderate cold. Jupiter has a natural connection with the melting processes of all other metals. The more it resembles another metal, the easier it is for them to join together. Similar things interact more smoothly and naturally than those that are very different. Something distant will not affect or influence something else strongly. Similarly, distant things are neither feared nor desired, no matter how powerful they might be.

This explains why people do not strive to reach higher realms of creation—they seem too far away, and their greatness is beyond human understanding. Likewise, lower realms are not feared, since people are distant from them and unaware of the suffering they contain. Because of this, spirits from the underworld are considered insignificant. The farther away something is, the less valuable it appears, while things close to us are given more importance. Each thing changes based on its place, becoming better or transforming according to where it belongs, as shown by many examples.

Jupiter is farther away from Mars and Venus but closer to the Sun (Sol) and Moon (Luna). Because of this, Jupiter contains more qualities similar to gold and silver. The closer it is to Sol and Luna, the more beautiful, powerful, visible, and valuable it becomes—far more so than a distant object. On the other hand, the farther something is, the less value it seems to hold, and things nearby are always favored over distant ones. As something nearby becomes clearer, what is farther away becomes hidden. As an alchemist, you must seriously consider how you can move Jupiter to a distant place occupied by Sol and Luna and bring Sol and Luna closer to where Jupiter is now. The goal is to have Sol and Luna present before your eyes in their full physical forms, just as Jupiter is.

There are practical methods for changing metals from imperfection to perfection. First, mix the metals together. Then, separate the pure parts from the impure. This process is simply one of transformation, carefully guided by proper alchemical work. Take note that Jupiter contains a significant amount of gold and some silver. If you combine it with Saturn and Luna, Luna will increase in its presence and strength.

•••

# Concerning Mars
# and His Properties

The six hidden metals have cast out the seventh, making it solid and giving it little power while making it heavy and hard. In doing so, they have transferred their own hardness and ability to solidify into this new body. However, they have kept their color, ability to melt, and noble qualities for themselves.

It is difficult and takes great effort to turn an ordinary man into a prince or king. But Mars, with a strong and aggressive nature, takes control and seizes the throne. Even so, he must stay alert, guarding against unexpected traps that could capture him off-guard. It is also important to consider how Mars can rise to power and take the place of the king, while Sol, Luna, and Saturn take over the role that Mars once held.

• • •

# Concerning Venus
# and Its Properties

The other six metals have transformed Venus into an external body by giving it their color and melting properties. To fully understand this, we should use some examples to show how something obvious can become hidden, and how something hidden can be made physically visible through the use of fire. Anything that can burn can naturally change its form through fire, turning into lime, soot, ash, glass, colors, stone, or earth. This earth can, in turn, be reshaped into new metallic bodies.

If a metal is burned or weakened by rust, it can regain its flexibility and strength through the careful application of fire.

•••

# Concerning The Nature And Proper- Ties op Saturn

Saturn speaks of himself in this way: "The other six metals have cast me out as their examiner. They have pushed me away from their spiritual state and given me a physical, perishable body as my dwelling, making me into something they are not and have no desire to become. My six brothers are spiritual in nature, and whenever I am placed in the fire, they enter my body and are destroyed along with me—except for Sol and Luna. These two are purified and made more noble by my waters. My spirit is like water, softening the rigid and frozen bodies of my brothers. However, my body is drawn toward the earth, and anything that enters into me takes on the same nature, becoming part of a single unified body through us.

It would do the world little good to know, or even believe, what lies hidden within me and what I am capable of achieving. It would be more valuable for the world to discover what I can do with myself. By abandoning the complex methods of the alchemists and focusing only on what I possess within me, people could find what I am truly able to accomplish. Within me lies the cold stone, a type of water that causes the spirits of the six metals to freeze together, creating the essence of the seventh metal. This process supports the transformation of Sol and Luna."

There are two types of antimony. One is the common black variety, which purifies Sol when it is melted within it. This black antimony has the closest connection to Saturn. The second type is white and is also known as magnesia or bismuth. It shares a strong connection with Jupiter, and when mixed with the black antimony, it increases the power of Luna.

● ● ●

# Concerning Luna And The Properties Thereof

The attempt to transform Luna into Saturn or Mars is no easier than turning Mercury, Jupiter, Mars, Venus, or Saturn into Luna with great success. It is not useful to change something perfect into something imperfect; instead, the goal is to transform the imperfect into the perfect. Still, it is important to understand what Luna is made of and where it originates. Anyone who cannot figure this out will not be able to create Luna.

So, what exactly is Luna? It is one of the seven metals, standing as the seventh. It exists externally as a physical, material substance, but within it, the other six metals are spiritually hidden. These six spiritual metals cannot exist on their own without a physical metal to contain them. Similarly, a physical metal cannot exist without these six spiritual elements. All seven metals can mix easily when melted together, but this kind of mixture is not enough to create Sol or Luna. Even when combined, each metal retains its own nature—either remaining stable in the fire or being burned away by it.

For example, if you mix Mercury, Jupiter, Saturn, Mars, Venus, Sol, and Luna into a single mass, the result will not be a transformation of the other metals into Sol or Luna. Even though they all melt together, each keeps its own essence. This is how physical mixtures work. However, when it comes to the spiritual mixture and unity of metals, it is important to understand that no separation or destruction of the spirit is truly possible. Spiritual elements cannot exist without physical bodies. Even if a body is destroyed and transformed a hundred times, the spirit within will always gain a new, more noble form. This process is the transformation of metals from one level to another—moving from a lesser form to a higher one, such as Luna. From there, the metal can be perfected into Sol, the brightest and most royal of all metals.

It is true, as mentioned before, that the six metals will always generate a seventh from within themselves, revealing it clearly in its true form.

One might ask: If Luna, like all metals, comes from the other six, what are its properties and nature? The answer is that no other metal besides Luna can be formed from the combination of Saturn, Mercury, Jupiter, Mars, Venus, and Sol. Each of these metals contributes two key qualities to Luna, making a total of twelve virtues. These twelve virtues represent the spirit of Luna, and each metal offers something unique to its composition.

Luna gains liquidity and its bright white color from Mercury, along with influences from the zodiac signs Aquarius and Pisces. It receives its whiteness and resistance to fire from Jupiter, along with traits from Sagittarius and Taurus. From Mars, along with Cancer and Aries, Luna gets its hardness and clear, ringing sound. From Venus, along with Gemini and Libra, Luna gains the ability to solidify. From Saturn, along with Virgo and Scorpio, Luna inherits a consistent body and weight. Finally, from Sol, with influences from Leo and Virgo, Luna receives its pure, spotless nature and strong resistance to fire.

This is the essence of Luna's spiritual and physical qualities. It is a combination of the six metals and their virtues, reflecting both wisdom and the natural order of exaltation, briefly summarized for understanding.

It is also important to explain what kind of body metallic spirits take on during their initial creation through the influence of the heavens. When a miner crushes a seemingly worthless stone, he melts it down, corrupts it, and completely breaks it apart with fire. During this process of destruction, the metallic spirit takes on a new body—one that is stronger and more refined. Instead of being brittle, it becomes soft and flexible.

Then the alchemist steps in, further corrupting, breaking down, and carefully refining this metallic body. Through this process, the spirit within the metal takes on an even more perfect form, revealing itself more clearly—unless it is Sol or Luna, which are already perfected. At last, the spirit and the body of the metal become fully united. They are now protected from the effects of ordinary fire and have reached a state where they cannot be corrupted.

• • •

# Concerning The Nature of Sol And Its Properties

The seventh metal, after the six spiritual ones, is Sol, which is purely fire in its nature. Outwardly, it is the most beautiful, brilliant, clear, and noticeable of all metals. It also has the heaviest and most uniform body. This is because it holds within itself the frozen essence of the other six metals, combining them into one solid form. Sol's ability to melt comes from either the heat of fire or the hidden influence of Mercury, along with the zodiac signs Pisces and Aquarius, that exist spiritually within it. We can see proof of this because Mercury blends effortlessly with Sol, almost as if in an embrace.

However, after Sol melts and the fire's heat is removed, cold takes over, causing it to harden. To make Sol solid and stable, it requires the essence of the other five metals—Jupiter, Saturn, Mars, Venus, and Luna—each of which contributes its cold nature.

Because of this, Sol is difficult to keep in liquid form without the constant heat of fire. Mercury cannot provide enough heat on its own to keep Sol melted, nor can it resist the coldness of the other five metals. Mercury's natural role is simply to stay in liquid form and flow, not to harden or make anything solid.

Heat and life belong to the same nature, bringing movement and fluidity, while cold brings hardness, stillness, and the absence of life, which can be compared to death. For instance, the six cold metals—Jupiter, Saturn, Mars, Venus, Luna, and even Venus again—can only be melted by the heat of fire. Snow and ice, being cold, will only cause things to harden further. Once a metal melted by fire cools, the cold seizes it, making it solid and frozen in place.

As for Mercury, in order to remain fluid and full of life, it depends on heat, not cold. Anyone who claims Mercury lives through cold and moisture misunderstands nature and follows common but mistaken beliefs. The truth is that life comes from warmth and fire, while cold brings death. Sol's fire is pure—it is not a living fire, but it is solid and contains the colors of sulfur, a perfect blend of yellow and red.

The five cold metals—Jupiter, Mars, Saturn, Venus, and Luna—each give Sol part of their nature. They contribute solidity through coldness, color through fire, hardness through dryness, weight through moisture, and sound through brightness. Gold, which is Sol's material form, cannot be burned or destroyed by ordinary earthly fire. This is because one fire cannot burn another fire; instead, adding fire to fire only makes it stronger.

The celestial fire we receive from the Sun on Earth is not the same as the fire in heaven or the fire we know on Earth. The fire from the Sun, when it reaches us, becomes cold and frozen—it forms the body of the Sun as we experience it. Therefore, earthly fire cannot overcome the fire of the Sun. Instead, the Sun's celestial fire melts objects, like snow or ice, but is never burned itself. Fire does not have the power to burn fire, because Sol is fire—its essence dissolved in the heavens but solidified here on Earth.

Gold is in its

  1 Celestial

Dissolved Essence three

   2 Elementary} and Fluid fold
   3 Metallic is Corporeal.

• • •

# Part II
## GOD AND NATURE DO NOTHING IN VAIN

The eternal nature of all things, existing beyond time, with no beginning or end, is always at work. It operates even in places where no hope can be found. It accomplishes what seems impossible. What once appeared beyond belief or hope reveals itself as truth in a marvelous and unexpected way.

...

# Note on Mercurius Vivus

Whatever gives a white color carries the essence of life and the qualities of light, which naturally bring life into being. In contrast, anything that produces blackness shares the nature of death, carrying the qualities of darkness and the forces that lead to death. The earth, with its cold nature, symbolizes this hardness, as it solidifies and fixes things. A house, for example, is always lifeless, but the person who lives inside it is alive. If you can understand the power of this idea, you have gained mastery.

Tested liquefactive powder: Burn the fat of verbena.

Recipe: Four ounces of saltpeter, half as much sulfur, and one ounce of tartar. Mix them and melt.

• • •

and Luna

# What Is to Be Thought
# Concerning The
# Congelation Of Mercury

Trying to solidify Mercury and turn it into Luna, while also refining it through great effort, is a waste of time. This process only leads to the loss of the Sol and Luna already present within Mercury. There is a much simpler and quicker way to transform Mercury into Luna, without the need for freezing or excessive labor. This method minimizes waste and saves effort, making it possible to create silver and gold with ease.

Anyone can learn this alchemical process since it is straightforward and simple. By using it, one can produce large amounts of silver and gold in a short time. Long, complicated explanations are unnecessary—most people prefer clear instructions. So, follow these steps, and you will create Sol and Luna, which will bring you wealth. Pay close attention as I explain this process briefly. Keep these instructions well in mind so that, by working with Saturn, Mercury, and Jupiter, you can produce Sol and Luna.

There is no easier or more effective method in alchemy, and it requires very little effort to master. The process for making Sol and Luna is so fast that no further books or detailed lessons are needed—writing more about it would be as pointless as documenting last year's snow.

• • •

# Concerning The Receipts of Alchemy

What, then, should we say about the recipes used in alchemy, along with the many different tools and vessels? These include furnaces, glassware, jars, waters, oils, lime, sulfur, salts, saltpeter, alum, vitriol, chrysocolla, copper greens, black inks, orpiment, green vitriol, white lead, red earth, thucia, wax, lutum sapientiae (the clay of wisdom), ground glass, verdigris, soot, eggshells, crocus of Mars, soap, crystal, chalk, arsenic, antimony, red lead, elixirs, lazurite, gold leaf, sal ammoniac, calamine stone, magnesia, Armenian bole, and many other substances.

Moreover, the steps involved—such as fermentation, digestion, testing, dissolving, cementing, filtering, refining, burning, distilling, purifying, and more— fill alchemical books to the brim. Then there are the materials drawn from herbs, roots, seeds, woods, stones, animals, worms, bone dust, snail shells, other shells, and pitch. Many of these things, however, only make the work more complicated. Even if Sol and Luna could be made with them, they would slow down the process rather than help it. The truth is that the art of creating Sol and Luna is not learned from these things. Therefore, they can be ignored, as they do not help when working with the five metals to make Sol and Luna.

Someone might ask, "What is the quick and easy way to create Sol and Luna, without unnecessary effort?" The answer is that this process has already been explained clearly and thoroughly in the Seven Canons. There is no point in trying to teach it to someone who does not grasp these Canons, as it would be difficult to convince them that this knowledge can be understood, though it must be approached in a hidden way rather than openly.

**The art is this:** Once you have created heaven, or the sphere of Saturn, and allowed its life to flow across the earth, place upon it the planets—whichever ones you choose—ensuring that Luna plays the smallest role. Let them run their course until Saturn, or heaven, has vanished entirely. At that point, the planets will remain lifeless, with their old, corruptible forms discarded. However, they will have gained new, perfect, and incorruptible bodies.

These new bodies are the spirit of heaven. From this spirit, the planets receive new forms and life, and they continue as they did before. Take this body, born from both life and earth, and keep it. It is Sol and Luna. Here, then, is the entire art, explained plainly and completely. If you still do not understand it, or have not practiced it, that is fine. It is better that this knowledge remains hidden and not revealed to everyone.

• • •

# How To Conjure The Crystal So That All Things May Be Seen In It

To conjure means nothing more than to observe something correctly, to know what it is, and to fully understand it. A crystal is a representation of the air. Whatever appears in the air—whether it moves or stays still—also appears as a reflection or wave within the crystal or mirror. This is because air, water, and crystal are the same in terms of how we see through them. They function like a mirror, showing a reversed image of whatever is reflected within them.

...

# Concerning The
# Heat of Mercury

Those who believe that Mercury is naturally cold and moist are mistaken. In truth, Mercury is warm and moist by nature, which is why it remains in a constant state of fluidity. If it were cold and moist, it would behave like frozen water, always solid and hard, requiring fire to melt it, as is the case with other metals. But Mercury doesn't need fire to become liquid. Its own natural heat keeps it fluid, giving it the ability to move freely, or "quick," meaning it cannot be killed, solidified, or frozen.

It is important to note that when the spirits of the seven metals, or however many are combined, meet fire, they compete with one another—especially Mercury. Each metal tries to display its powers and virtues, working to dominate the others through liquefaction and transformation. One metal will take on the life and properties of another, giving a new form and nature to the one it overtakes. The heat stirs the spirits or vapors of the metals to interact with each other, constantly changing one into another until they reach perfection and purity.

What, then, must be done to Mercury to remove its natural warmth and moisture, and replace them with extreme cold that will solidify, bind, and fully harden it? Follow this method: Take pure Mercury and seal it tightly in a silver container. Place this container in the middle of a jar filled with pieces of lead. Allow it to melt for twenty-four hours, or one full day. This process removes Mercury's hidden heat, adds external warmth, and introduces the coldness of Saturn and Luna, two planets with cold properties. This forces Mercury to freeze, solidify, and become firm.

It is important to understand that the cold needed to solidify Mercury is not the same as the cold we feel from snow or ice. Instead, this cold has a different quality—on the surface, there may even seem to be some warmth. Likewise, the heat that keeps Mercury fluid is not the same kind of heat we normally experience. Instead, Mercury can feel cool to the touch, which has led some scholars, who speak more than they understand, to wrongly conclude that Mercury is cold and moist. They mistakenly suggest that heat will solidify Mercury, but instead, heat makes it even more fluid, as they continue to discover at their own expense.

True alchemy, which teaches the only way to make Sol and Luna from the five imperfect metals, offers this principle: "Only from metals, within metals, by metals, and through metals can perfect metals be made." In some metals lies the essence of Luna, and in others, the essence of Sol.

• • •

# What Materials And Instruments Are Required in Alchemy

All you need are a foundry, bellows, tongs, hammers, cauldrons, jars, and small refining dishes made from beech ashes. After gathering these tools, introduce the metals—Saturn, Jupiter, Mars, Sol, Venus, Mercury, and Luna. Let the process run its course, finishing with Saturn.

...

# The Method of Seeking Minerals

The hope of finding metals within the earth and stones is very uncertain, and the effort required is immense. However, since this is the most direct way to obtain them, it should not be dismissed but highly praised. This desire to seek metals should be encouraged, just as the natural desire for marriage in youth and adulthood is accepted. Just as bees are drawn to roses and other flowers to create honey and wax, so too should people—apart from greed or selfish ambition—seek metals within the earth. Whoever does not search for them is unlikely to find them. God grants not only gold and silver to some but also poverty, hardship, and suffering.

Some people, however, are given special knowledge of metals and minerals, enabling them to discover easier ways to create gold and silver. These methods are faster than digging and smelting, allowing them to extract precious metals from their original forms. This applies not only to things found underground but also to metals refined from imperfect minerals. Gold and silver (Sol and Luna) can be made from any of the five metals—Mercury, Jupiter, Saturn, Mars, and Venus—although some are easier to work with than others. Sol and Luna can be made more easily from Mercury, Saturn, and Jupiter, while it is more difficult to create them from Mars and Venus, though it is still possible with the addition of existing Sol and Luna. For example, Luna can be produced from Magnesium and Saturn, while pure Sol can be made from Jupiter and Cinnabar.

A skilled alchemist, through careful thought and study, can perfect the transformation of metals better than by relying on the movements of the twelve zodiac signs or the seven planets. It is unnecessary to follow these celestial movements, whether they indicate favorable or unfavorable days, good or bad planetary influences. These things neither help nor hinder the process of natural alchemy. If you have a working process, you can perform the operation whenever you choose. However, if something is missing from your method or understanding, no alignment of stars or planets will make up for it.

Metals that remain buried in the earth for too long not only rust but can also transform into natural stones over time, though this is known to very few.

In fact, old coins from ancient times, bearing various images, are sometimes found in the earth. These coins were originally made of metal but, through the slow transformation of nature, have turned into stone.

• • •

# What Alchemy Is

Alchemy is the deliberate effort to change one type of metal into another. Each person, using their own understanding, can find the best path and discover the truth, as truth is revealed to those who pursue it with dedication. It is essential to understand both stars and stones because the spirit of all stones is linked to the stars. Sol (the Sun) and Luna (the Moon), representing celestial bodies, are also connected to a single stone. The stones of the earth originate from these celestial stones. Through fire, purification, and separation, these earthly stones are made bright and pure, much like their celestial counterparts. The entire earth is made from a mixture of materials that have solidified into a stony mass resting within the larger sphere of the universe.

Precious stones found on earth are the closest in perfection to the heavenly stones. These earthly stones possess purity, beauty, brilliance, strength, and resistance to fire, just like celestial stones. However, they are often found in rough environments, and most people mistakenly believe these stones were created exactly where they were found. They assume that these stones were simply polished and traded for their beauty, color, and value. A brief description of these stones follows:

The **Emerald** is a transparent green stone. It is said to improve eyesight and memory and protect purity. If the person carrying it loses their purity, the stone will lose its perfection.

The **Adamant** is a black crystal, also called Evax, known for bringing joy to those who carry it. It is dark, with a metallic color, and is the hardest of all stones. However, it can dissolve in goat's blood. It rarely grows larger than a hazelnut.

The **Magnet** is a stone made of iron that attracts iron to itself.

The **Pearl** is not truly a stone since it forms inside seashells. It is white and grows within living creatures, like fish or mollusks, which makes it different from typical stones.

The **Jacinth** is a yellow, transparent stone. Its name also refers to a flower, which legend says was once a man.

The **Sapphire** is a stone with a heavenly color and is considered connected to celestial qualities.

The **Ruby** glows with an intense red color.

The **Carbuncle** is a solar stone that shines as brightly as the sun itself.

The **Coral** is a stone that can be white or red. It forms in the sea, growing like a plant or shrub. When exposed to air, it hardens and becomes fireproof.

The **Chalcedony** is a stone with mixed colors, sitting between transparency and opacity, often with cloudy or liver-colored patterns. It is considered the least valuable of the precious stones.

The **Topaz** is known to shine at night and is found among rocks.

The **Amethyst** is a stone with a purple or blood-red hue.

The **Chrysoprasus** shines like fire at night and resembles gold during the day.

The **Crystal** is a transparent white stone that looks like ice. It forms from the essence of other stones through extraction and purification.

The key to understanding these stones lies in knowing their origins and connection to metals. The truth is that metals are the most refined part of common stones. They contain elements like oil, fat, and grease, but they remain impure and imperfect as long as they are mixed within the stones. To create perfect metals, these elements must be identified, separated, and extracted from the stones through a process of melting and refining. Once purified, the substance becomes a metal comparable to the stars, which are themselves like separated stones from the heavens.

Those who study metals and minerals must be guided by reason and intelligence. They should not limit themselves to exploring only the known metals buried deep within mountains. Often, valuable metals are found closer to the earth's surface, while deeper layers may not yield the same quality. Every stone—whether a large boulder or a simple rock—must be examined carefully, for even a stone that seems worthless might contain hidden value, sometimes more valuable than livestock. The place where a stone is found does not always determine its true worth, as the influence of the sky plays a role in its formation. Even common earth, dust, or sand can contain traces of gold or silver, and those who look carefully will notice this.

• • •

# The End

# Thank you for Reading

**You've Just Read a Piece of the Greatest Library Ever Rebuilt**

Thank you for reading.

This book is one of thousands we're restoring, reimagining, and translating as part of the **Modern Library of Alexandria** — a global movement to preserve and share humanity's most important ideas.

What was once lost to fire and time is now rising again — not just as memory, but as living, breathing knowledge, freely accessible to all.

**What You Can Do Next:**

· **Keep Reading.**

  Discover more legendary works — in beautiful print, audiobook, or digital form — at LibraryofAlexandria.com.

· **Build Your Own Library.**

  Every title is available as a paperback, hardcover, or collectible boxset — at true printing cost. Craft a personal library worthy of display.

· **Spread the Light.**

  Share this book. Tell others about the movement. Help us translate every timeless work into every language, so no reader is ever left behind.

By finishing this book, you've already taken part in something extraordinary.

**Join us at LibraryofAlexandria.com**

Together, we're rebuilding the greatest library the world has ever known.

With appreciation,
**The Modern Library of Alexandria Team**

**Visit:**

**www.libraryofalexandria.com**

**Or scan the code below:**